CHORAL THERAPY

TECHNIQUES AND EXERCISES
FOR THE CHURCH CHOIR

Lloyd Pfautsch

Abingdon Press
Nashville

CHORAL THERAPY
Techniques and Exercises for the Church Choir

Copyright © 1994 by Abingdon Press

This book is printed on acid-free, recycled paper.

Library of Congress Cataloging-in-Publication Data

Pfautsch, Lloyd.
  Choral therapy : techniques and exercises for the church choir / Lloyd Pfautsch.
    p.   cm.
  ISBN 0-687-06510-0
  1. Choral singing—Instruction and study. 2. Church music—Instruction and study.
MT875.P44   1994
782.5'143—dc20   93-39299
                                              CIP
                                              MN

02 03 — 10 9 8 7 6

MANUFACTURED IN THE UNITED STATES OF AMERICA

CHORAL THERAPY

To my former students
with great appreciation for their wonderful voices,
probing questions, patient cooperation,
and constant stimulation

Contents

List of Figures

Preface

When Gary Alan Smith, the music editor at Abingdon Press, asked me if I would consider writing a brief book on voice that might be of assistance to church choir conductors, I thought, "How could I turn down such an opportunity, and one extended by a former student?" While pagination would be limited, the content was not, except for the limitation implicit in the title of the book.

Actually, the title, *Choral Therapy,* is a succinct way of stating what the content of this book attempts to provide. Therefore, I hope that this book will be a service to church choir conductors (or any choral conductors). I also hope that it may assist them as they work with singers, so that the voices benefit from the therapeutic treatment and guidance provided by the conductors.

Since I have been a conductor of church choirs and university choirs, a singer and voice teacher, and an author of books on English diction and rehearsal technique during the past fifty years, I concluded that there was much I could share from that experience. For many years, I also taught a class in Vocal and Choral Techniques. For some conductors, this book may be a review; for other conductors it may confirm what they are already doing; while for still another group it may provide some new and diverse ideas or suggestions.

As a singer, I had learned much from my teachers and from conductors with whom I had sung. As a voice teacher, I had expanded my understanding of the human instrument and my appreciation of the myriad problems I encountered in trying to improve the tone production of singers. I also developed pedagogical procedures to free and refine voice production, as I borrowed from my teachers, read many books on vocal pedagogy, observed and responded to workshops on voice—but mainly as I created vocalises to solve various problems presented by students.

As a conductor, I employed my vocal pedagogy in rehearsals, not as obviously or as extensively as in private lessons, but more indirectly. This called for both creative use of vocal pedagogy and constant experimentation. Early in my career, it became obvious to me that this process of appropriation and experimentation would be endless. I also observed other conductors in rehearsal and analyzed what they did to achieve good vocal production. I learned very quickly that borrowing without analysis and an understanding of what another conductor was doing is simply imitation and could be both dangerous and ineffective. It also discourages personal development of creative imagination and experimentation. Just because a certain vocal technique worked for another conductor did not mean it would work for me. But after analyzing why a technique was effective, it might become possible to use that understanding and achieve comparable results with my own method and manner of communication. I shared this conclusion with my conducting students throughout the years in the hope that they would not imitate me, but rather gain an understanding of why I did what I did to achieve the sounds of my ensembles.

In addition to this vocal and choral experience, I have also drawn from the Vocal and Choral Techniques class mentioned earlier. Since it was a course lasting one semester, I have obviously included only data from that course that is applicable in this book. Thus, this book shares what I have found to be of assistance to me as I sought to provide choral therapy for my singers.

I am indebted to all who sang in the various choral ensembles I conducted, to the voice students I was privileged to teach, to the many members of conducting and related choral classes, and to the long line of graduate choral conducting majors, all of whom endured my developing (and changing) pedagogical procedures. Their probing questions contributed greatly to the ongoing refining process, and their splendid cooperation made possible the necessary and important experimentation. A special word of appreciation is extended to Gary Alan Smith and Abingdon Press, since their invitation encouraged me to record my thoughts concerning choral therapy. And finally, I must pay tribute to my wife, Edith, who monitored my work on this book with critical acumen and asked questions that frequently required clarification of material for clearer communication.

Lloyd Pfautsch
Dallas, TX

Chapter One:
The Choir Conductor

The Conductor's Instrument

All church choir conductors have to accept broad responsibilities when rehearsing with those who sing under their direction. However, one of the most demanding responsibilities is working with the voices of choir members. Every choir conductor is dependent on singers and the proper use of their voices.

The singer's voice is the human instrument. The combination of voices making up a choir is the conductor's instrument. It has been suggested that conductors are the only performers who have to practice on their instrument in public. During this practice, the choral conductor is also a voice teacher. As this instrument is heard, the conductor must deal with an assortment of personalities, ages, backgrounds, temperaments, experiences and training as singers. This mixture can change from church to church, region to region, year to year, and even week to week. Perhaps the only constant expectation is the variety making up the sound of any choir.

The Conductor as Voice Teacher

Much is expected of a choir director when working with this instrument. Here is a list of some of the expectations:

1. The conductor should have a good educational background in music.

2. The conductor should have some vocal training. One does not need to be an excellent singer to be a good choir director. Such ability and training can be of great value, but not every good singer becomes a good choir conductor (or even a good voice teacher!). However, learning how to use one's own singing voice correctly is

important to every choir conductor even though the conductor never sings as a soloist.

3. The conductor should have experience as a choir member since it will enhance an appreciation for all that is involved when singing in a choir.

4. The conductor should be aware of the fact that for most people who sing in a church choir the conductor will be their only voice teacher. There will always be some members of the choir who have studied voice, but they will generally be few in number.

5. The conductor must be willing to accept the responsibility for the vocal training of the choir members.

6. The conductor must not allow any personal vocal limitations or inadequacies to deter serving as a voice teacher for the choir.

7. The conductor must continually expand on and refine personal vocal training and understanding of the voice so that vocal problems heard in the choir's sound can be analyzed and corrections or refinements suggested.

8. The conductor must be able to explain to the singers what is involved in the problem as well as in the correction and refinement process. For example, the conductor should avoid merely saying that the tone quality is not good or that the technique is incorrect. Instead, the conductor should explain (or demonstrate) why the singer is not producing the correct sound and what can be done to improve it.

9. It is also important that the conductor be able and willing to demonstrate good vocal production. This does not require beauty of sound, but merely correctness of vocal technique.

10. When providing this voice training for the singers, the conductor should cultivate the ability to interact with them in such a way that they feel encouraged rather than discouraged. Most singers will be able to sense and feel the differences in their vocal production and will appreciate the assistance given by the conductor. The differences can be less tension, greater ease in singing, and more satisfaction and enjoyment when singing.

Advantages of Singing in a Choir

1. The choir is afforded the opportunity to serve the music ministry of the church.

2. The singers can experience a sense of satisfaction and fulfillment as they participate in worship and provide contributions to the ministry of worship.

3. Singing can be a healthful activity since it involves extensive use of the lungs and helps increase their capacity.

4. The speaking voice will be helped since singing is often described as speech intoned.

5. The guidance provided by a conductor/teacher involves the elimination of bad habits and the cultivation of good habits.

6. The development of good singing habits can enable a choir to sing a wider variety of anthems.

7. These good habits make singing more enjoyable and satisfying as bad habits and resulting tenseness are relieved.

8. Under the guidance of the conductor/teacher, singers can develop proper use of the singing voice.

9. Singing in the choir can assist the development of musical knowledge and understanding.

10. The disciplines of the choir rehearsal can help singers maintain good memory and concentration.

11. Singing in the choir often enlarges the appreciation and understanding of biblical texts and religious poetry.

12. The experience of singing in the choir can enhance the enjoyment of professional singers and other choral ensembles.

13. Singing in the choir can awaken an awareness of personal responsibilities for good singing within a cooperating group of singers.

Chapter Two:
Producing Vocal Sound

Breath Control

O ne of the first responsibilities a conductor has as a voice
teacher is helping the singers understand the role the breath
plays in singing. Most people use the breathing mechanism
correctly when they laugh, shout, cough, whisper, or sneeze, but they
often fail to use it correctly when they speak, and especially when
they sing. As has been said earlier, singing is speech intoned. Most
untrained singers do not realize that the proper use of breath is
important and necessary. Singing requires a more vital use of breath
than speaking. Figure 1 shows the human instrument with basic ter-
minology. (See the Glossary for definitions of the terms.)

Fig. 1: The human instrument

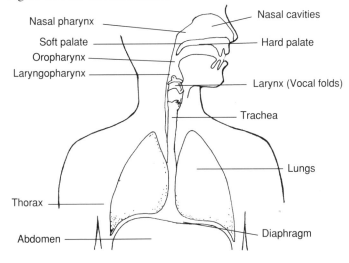

Nasal pharynx

Nasal cavities

Soft palate

Hard palate

Oropharynx

Laryngopharynx

Larynx (Vocal folds)

Trachea

Lungs

Thorax

Abdomen

Diaphragm

Fig. 2: Lower ribs and abdomen

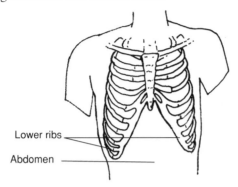

Since tone production in singing depends on how the breath is used, most untrained singers need to learn how to use the breath. A good way to make singers aware of the source of breath support is to ask them to make a fist with either hand. They should inhale and bring their lips together in a tight position against the fist as if they were playing a brass instrument. Then have them blow against the fist, making it difficult for the air to be released. They should feel a tightening and an expansion of the abdominal muscles just below the rib cage.

Fig. 3: "X" showing position of the lips

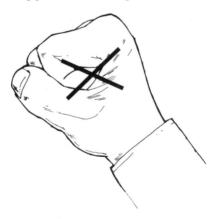

In addition, have the singers articulate the consonant *z* and continue the sound (*zzzzzzzzzz*), the consonant *s* (*ssssssssss*, like hissing), and then the consonant *v* (*vvvvvvvvvv*). The consonants can also be repeated five times (*z, z, z, z, z; s, s, s, s, s;* and *v, v, v, v, v*). Do not use a vowel sound like *zah*. Use only the consonant sound.

Another way to achieve a similar result is to ask the singers to say or sing the word *hook* and stop the outward flow of air at the beginning of the consonant *k*. Use also the words *hip* and *zip*, stopping the outward flow of air at the closure of the lips. In both the *k* and *p*, hold the start of the consonant, and after a few seconds of holding the air in, finally release it. Singers need to be made aware of the need for control and capacity of breath. The following exercises can be used in warming up a choir.

1. Ask the singers to extend their arms in front of their bodies, then extend the arms to the side, and finally move them up behind the head, where they will clasp their hands against the back of the head. This will help posture by keeping the shoulders and upper chest high. It also inhibits the use of the chest primarily for breathing and forces the singers to breathe from the abdomen and lower rib area. When the breath is taken, the inhalation forces the diaphragm down and expands the lower ribs along with the abdomen.

2. As the conductor counts, the singers can be instructed to take short inhalations through the nostrils on each count. The director lets the singers know how long the counting will be, for example, one (breathe), two (breathe), and so on up to ten. The singers are then directed to release the air with a hissing or buzzing sound as the conductor again counts from one to ten. Singers should reach their full capacity at the count of ten while inhaling, and also be at the end of the breath supply at ten when hissing or buzzing. The count should change constantly. Count from one to fifteen, one to six, one to twelve, one to four, one to nine, and so on. Changing the count is important because this exercise will help develop control, capacity, and the focused use of breath. It also develops the muscles involved in that control, capacity, and use, the ability to breathe quickly and rhythmically, and the ability to sustain phrases of different length.

3. Vocalises can also be used to help develop capacity and control in supporting and sustaining tone production.

Ex. 1

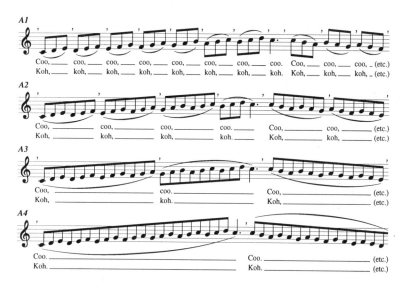

Ex. 2

Ex. 3

Ex. 4

In each of the exercises in Examples 1 to 4 move not only step-wise from one key to the next, but move around (for example, C, E, B, F, D-flat, G, B-flat, D, A-flat, and so on). This will help develop the ear and also eliminate the danger of increased tension when moving diatonically. The exercise A1 will obviously be limited in range and related to comfortable ranges for each section.

The singer must always begin with a full breath and use only the amount necessary to sing the prescribed sequence of notes. It is important that the singers breathe in rhythm related to whatever tempo has been set by the conductor. The tempo should remain the same throughout the exercise if the emphasis is on increasing the capacity. When repeating this exercise, the tempo should vary if the emphasis is on learning how to take the breath with different tempi.

Using an initial *k, z,* or *y* before the vowel sound forces the singers to involve the breath as the initiator of singing (and speech). Changing the vowels is important since singing involves a variety of vowel sounds that vary in accordance with their appearances in syllables or words.

Ex. 5: *Messiah* - "His Yoke Is Easy"

These exercises will assist the singers in developing their breath control and capacity and demonstrate the important relation of breath to tone production. They can be used during the warm-up period, but not all need to be used at every rehearsal. Portions can be used each time. The development of breath capacity and control is a lengthy process and no singer ever arrives at the point where breathing exercises are not needed. Some will need more and others less. However, most church choir members will always need breathing exercises.

What has been done in these exercises can be applied when working on the music by asking each singer to mark the places in their music where a breath is to be taken.

It is also essential that the conductor's preparatory gestures help the singers breathe. The breath must be taken rhythmically in relation to the tempo of the anthem being sung! This is especially important at the end of a phrase and at the beginning of the next phrase. (See Ex. 5.)

Ex. 6: *Messiah* - "And He Shall Purify"

In the first measure, sopranos must breathe on the second beat—that is, on the eighth rest (see Ex. 6). In measure 2, a breath will be necessary before the word *and*, which means that the breath must be taken on the fourth beat. The same is true for the basses in the fifth and sixth measures.

Ex. 7: *Messiah* - "And He Shall Purify"

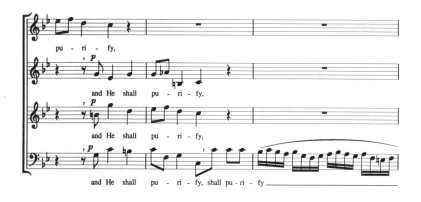

In the first measure, altos, tenors, and basses take a breath on the second beat—that is, on the eighth rest (see Ex. 7). However, in the next measure, a breath by the basses will be necessary between the end of the word *purify* and the start of the word *shall*. It must be taken more quickly than in the first measure, but it should be done rhythmically so that the second phrase entrance is not delayed.

Ex. 8: *Messiah* - "Worthy Is the Lamb"

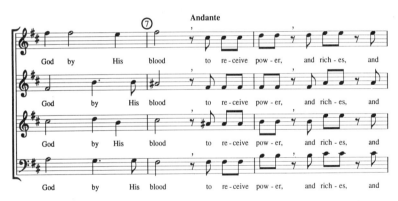

At the beginning of this chorus, the breath should be taken on the first beat of the measure and at the *largo* tempo (see Ex. 8). However, at measure 7 the breath must be taken faster for two reasons: (1) the entrance is on an eighth note; and (2) the tempo is faster, or *andante*.

Ex. 9: *Messiah* - "Hallelujah"

In the famous "Hallelujah" chorus (measures 4-7), the breath is taken on the fourth beat of measure 3 and on the fourth beat of measure 4 at whatever tempo the conductor determines (see Ex. 9). In measure 5, the breath is also taken on the fourth beat, faster yet in tempo because of the eighth note entrance. The same is true for the two entrances in measure 6. The conductor must time the preparatory beat or alerting movement of the cueing gesture so that the singers' breathing will have correct duration and rhythm.

While practicing the preparatory beat, it is helpful if conductors themselves breathe at varying tempi. This will enable them to understand how the singers must breathe and how to time the preparatory gesture to make breathing time both possible and accurate. The breathing of singers can be helped or hindered by how a conductor times the preparatory movement. Empathetic involvement by the conductor with the singer is most important! Failure to do this can inhibit and delay breathing by the singers. Conductors should help the singers breathe correctly in the conducting gestures involving the cueing of entrances.

As an anthem is sung, if the tone quality lacks vitality, ask the singers to sing their line using only *zah, zoh, zee,* or *zoo.* The use of the consonant *z* is of utmost importance since it forces the singers to use the breath to support the subsequent vowel.

Ex. 10: *Messiah* - "Glory to God"

Ex. 11:
Then sing:

Zoh, Zee, Zoo, Zod,   Zoh, Zee, Zoo, Zod, Zihn, Zuh, Zigh - Zest.

The use of the consonant *z* forces the singers to use the breath to start the tone and helps them connect the breath with the vowel sound. This can be done at any time breath support is inadequate and needs to be vitalized. While this problem can arise when singing *forte,* it is more prevalent when singing *piano.* Many singers assume that singing *piano* does not require as much breath support as singing *forte,* and as a result fail to use the breath properly. Actually, breath support is usually more important when singing *piano* so that the vitality of tone is not lost.

Posture

One final word about breath support. Posture is very important, whether sitting or standing to sing in a rehearsal. Since church choirs sit more than they stand, be sure that the choir members do not slouch while sitting, for this inhibits the proper and effective use of the breathing mechanism and thus impairs good singing. Church choir rehearsals are usually in the evening and at the end of a working day so it is easy for singers to have a relaxed attitude during rehearsals. However, they must be made to accept the necessity of good posture when rehearsing.

It is also advisable to have the choir stand frequently during a rehearsal to provide some relief from sitting, and to stress the importance of good posture while standing to sing. This posture should not be a ramrod erectness. To achieve the correct bearing, ask the singers to "stand tall" and then stand on their tiptoes several times before coming to rest with their feet flat on the floor. Another way is to use the breathing exercise #1 on page 17. After placing the hands against the back of the head, let them come down to the sides of the body without allowing the shoulders and upper chest to move. These procedures will assist singers in attaining the proper bearing and carriage of the body for singing.

Resonance

All singers must understand the role of resonance in singing. It is the conductor's responsibility to help them gain this understanding.

Poor tone quality is variously called throaty, strident, nasal, and so on, depending on the jargon used by a conductor. Singers may or may not understand the jargon, so explanations and sometimes demonstrations must be provided by the conductor. Many singers do not hear these variations of tone quality since the tone quality they produce seems "natural" to them. Indeed, it is natural since they have produced this sound for so many years, and have grown accustomed to what they hear and feel.

Throaty quality usually results from too much tension at the back of the tongue and in the oropharynx. (See Fig. 1 on page 15.) Strident tone quality usually involves excessive direction of the tone against the hard palate. A nasal tone quality uses too much of the head and nose resonating chambers.

The exercises shown in Example 12 can help to develop better use of the resonance potential in each singer.

Ex. 12

As with the previous exercises, vary the tonalities. Try to avoid stepwise movement when going from one key to the next. Move the keys around, for example, C, F, D, B, G, E, and so on. This exercise will improve the proper use of head resonance and help to eliminate the strident and throaty quality. The exercises in Example 13 have been useful in relieving throat tension:

Ex. 13

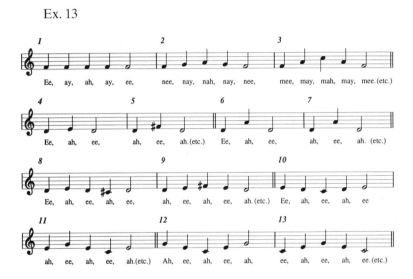

Both of these exercises can help eliminate too much nasal or head resonance. Once again, changing keys is desirable. The objective is the proper and coordinated use of the resonance potential and the elimination of unnecessary and excessive tension in tone production.

Chapter Three:
Considering Diction

In the preceding exercises in chapter 2, vowel sounds have been used repeatedly. In order to ensure that the singers produce clear and correct sounds, the conductor must consider the importance of diction. Unfortunately, there are mistaken assumptions about diction that include one or more of the following:

1. Since English is the native language for most American church choirs, not much work on diction is required. The singers will know how to produce the vowels and consonants, and the congregation will understand the text.

Response: Most Americans do not speak correct or clear English and present a conductor with a wide variety of colloquialisms and bad speech habits that become accentuated in singing.

2. If Latin or another language is used on rare occasions, very few in the choir and congregation will know whether it is sung correctly.

Response: Many choirs will have members who know the language and can provide guidance if the conductor is not capable of doing so. The conductor can also call in a language teacher to give guidance. There may be members of the congregation who know the foreign language and thus expect clarity.

3. The singers think they are producing good diction when they are singing.

Response: Of course they do, otherwise they would not be singing as they do! But that does not mean their diction is correct and clear. The conductor must maintain objectivity while making corrections and refinements without disparaging the efforts of the singers.

4. The conductor also thinks that the diction is clear and understandable.

Response: This is usually due to familiarity with the text prior to and during the rehearsing of the anthem. The conductor must listen as if it were the first time the text was being heard and be willing to take the time and make the effort necessary for refinement and clarity of the text.

5. Many anthems use familiar texts from the Bible or the hymnal so the congregation will understand the text even if the diction is not clear.

Response: While there is some truth in this statement, when the texts are familiar the congregation anticipates being able to hear and also understand the words. If they cannot, they will often complain. But the conductor should not assume that the congregation will compliment the choir's diction when it is clear and understood, for the congregation expects this or takes it for granted.

Vowel Sounds

In Figure 4 the symbols for the vowel sounds as indicated by the International Phonetic Association (IPA) appear in the brackets next to the key words and also in the brackets giving the phonetic spelling of the key words.

The vowel chart in Figure 5 will be helpful in understanding the sequence employed; the jaw, tongue, and lip movements; and the relationships of vowels making up diphthongs and triphthongs. The numbers in the parentheses that follow the numbers 8 to 13 indicate the position of the tongue and jaw behind the rounding of the lips; for example, "Her 11 (4)" means that the tongue and jaw are in the position required for sounding the *eh* vowel (ε as in *head*) behind the rounded lips, thus achieving the *uhr* vowel sound (ɜ as in *her*). In the list of diphthongs and triphthongs, the numbers, and the words in the brackets indicate which vowels (1 to 13) are used to produce the diphthongs and triphthongs.

VOWELS

Group One

Key Word	Phonetic Spelling
[i] heat	[hit]
[ɪ] hit	[hɪt]
[e] hate	[het]
[ɛ] head	[hɛd]
[æ] hat	[hæt]
[ʌ] hut	[hʌt]
[ə] patrol	[pətrol]
[ɑ] hot	[hɑt]

Group Two

Key Word	Phonetic Spelling
[ɒ] hod	[hɒd]
[ɔ] haw	[hɔ]
[o] hope	[hop]
[ɜ] her	[hɜ]
[ʊ] hook	[hʊk]
[u] hoot	[hut]

Group Three

Key Word	Phonetic Spelling
A. [ɑɪ] buy	[bɑɪ]
[ɔɪ] boy	[bɔɪ]
[ɛɪ] bay	[bɛɪ]
B. [ɪɜ] fear	[fɪɜ]
[ɛɜ] fair	[fɛɜ]
[ɑɜ] far	[fɑɜ]
[ɔɜ] for	[fɔɜ]
[oɜ] pore	[poɜ]
[ʊɜ] poor	[pʊɜ]
C. [ɑu] now	[nɑu]
[ou] no	[nou]
[iu] new	[niu]

Group Four

Key Word	Phonetic Spelling
[ɑɪɜ] tire	[tɑɪɜ]
[ɑuɜ] tower	[tɑuɜ]

Reprinted from *English Diction for the Singer* by Lloyd Pfautsch, Lawson-Gould Music Publisher, Inc. with permission.

Fig. 5:

VOWEL CHART

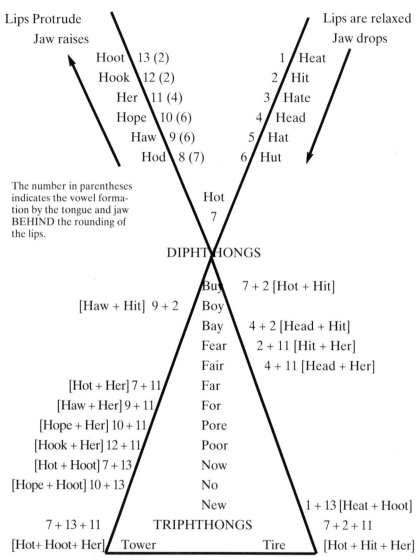

Lips Protrude
Jaw raises

Lips are relaxed
Jaw drops

Hoot	13 (2)		1	Heat
Hook	12 (2)		2	Hit
Her	11 (4)		3	Hate
Hope	10 (6)		4	Head
Haw	9 (6)		5	Hat
Hod	8 (7)		6	Hut

The number in parentheses indicates the vowel formation by the tongue and jaw BEHIND the rounding of the lips.

Hot
7

DIPHTHONGS

		Buy	7 + 2 [Hot + Hit]
[Haw + Hit] 9 + 2		Boy	
		Bay	4 + 2 [Head + Hit]
		Fear	2 + 11 [Hit + Her]
		Fair	4 + 11 [Head + Her]
[Hot + Her] 7 + 11		Far	
[Haw + Her] 9 + 11		For	
[Hope + Her] 10 + 11		Pore	
[Hook + Her] 12 + 11		Poor	
[Hot + Hoot] 7 + 13		Now	
[Hope + Hoot] 10 + 13		No	
		New	1 + 13 [Heat + Hoot]

7 + 13 + 11   **TRIPHTHONGS**   7 + 2 + 11
[Hot+ Hoot+ Her]   Tower   Tire   [Hot + Hit + Her]

Reprinted from *English Diction for the Singer* by Lloyd Pfautsch, Lawson-Gould Music Publishers, Inc. with permission.

Though most of the tone produced when singing involves vowel sounds, singing differs from speech in the following ways:

1. The duration of vowel sounds is much longer in singing than in speech except when assigned to notes of short duration in either a slow or fast tempo.

Ex. 14: *Messiah* - "Since by Man Came Death"

Since the tempo indication is *grave*, the vowel sounds in each word will be much longer than in speech (see Ex. 14).

Ex. 15: *Messiah* - "Let Us Break Their Bonds Asunder"

SHORT

Allegro e staccato

Since the tempo indication is *allegro e staccato,* the vowel sounds
will be very short and more like speech (see Ex. 15).

2. The pitch of the vowel varies greatly from pitches used in
speaking.

Ex. 16: *Messiah* - "And with His Stripes We Are Healed"

The setting of these words for the soprano line involves much
more pitch variation than the sopranos would use if they were speaking the text (see Ex. 16).

3. The range of vowel sound pitches is far greater in singing than
in speech.

When singing the phrase "for the Lord God Omnipotent" twice,
the tenor's range is from D below the staff to G above the staff,
while the range of the basses is from low G to D above the staff (see
Ex. 17). In Example 18, the sopranos not only have to sing a long
first vowel in the word *easy,* but they also cover more than an octave
range when singing the phrase "His yoke is easy."

Ex. 17: *Messiah* - "Hallelujah!"

Ex. 18: *Messiah* - "His Yoke Is Easy"

4. The volume of vowel sounds is often greater and sometimes softer in singing than in speech because of the dynamic markings provided by the composer (see Exx. 19 and 20).

Ex. 19: *Elijah* - "Help, Lord!" (Loud)

Ex. 20: *Elijah* - "Cast Thy Burden upon the Lord"

It is also important that a choir conductor understand that there is a relationship between vowel formation, range, and pitch.

Ex. 21: *Messiah* - "His Yoke Is Easy"

In Example 21, the vocal line for singers involves the use of pitches in the upper range of their voices. For this reason, slight adjustments must be made in the vowel formations. For example, when the sopranos and tenors sing the word *easy*, they will move to the *ih* (I as in *hit*) on the F and stay close to this vowel sound throughout the sixteenth notes. This will sound like an *e* (i as in *heat*) and will put them in the correct vowel position for the *ih* (I as in *hit*), the correct vowel sound for the unaccented second syllable. Avoid going to an *e* (i as in *heat*) in the second syllable, for *e* is not correct, and will accent the unaccented syllable, which must be negated to provide the proper syllabic nuance.

The higher each section of voices moves in their range, the more they should move toward the subsequent vowel on the vowel chart, that is, from 1 to 7 and from 13 to 7. (Note that on the vowel chart, the number in parentheses next to numbers 13 to 8 indicates the positions of the tongue and jaw behind the changing aperture of the lips.) To insist on a pure *e* vowel when the sopranos and tenors sing on or above the staff can result in tongue, jaw, and throat tension.

Most singers will naturally migrate away from the pure *e* vowel. But this needs to be moderated because: (1) they may migrate too far, possibly as far as *eh* (ε as in *head*), or (2) they may migrate to various vowel positions, with each singer having his or her own approximation of the correct vowel sound. The result will be a lack of uniformity of vowel sounds.

Experience and experimentation has taught this conductor that asking for the *e* (i) vowel usually elicits the *ih* (I) vowel, which sounds like the *e* vowel in the upper range. The same problem can be encountered when the altos and basses sing an *e* vowel in their upper range, and the same solution can be applied.

To prove this to your singers, have them sing and sustain what they consider to be an *e* vowel (i as in *heat*) on a high note beginning with the consonant *s*. As they are sustaining the vowel sound, tell them to add the consonant *t* as they release the sound. In most instances, they will hear the word *sit*. However, it is possible to hear among the singers the word *sate, set,* or *sat.* Be careful and considerate when you point out the differences. Do not chastise them for singing the wrong vowel. They think they are singing the right vowel. They are trying, but not succeeding. If you isolate each group and have them sing their own "variation" of the *e* vowel, it becomes obvious to all that there is a democratic process involved and that they are "voting" for different vowel sounds in an honest attempt to produce the correct vowel sound. The conductor should hear these differences and help the singers become aware not only of the differences, but also of how wonderful the vowel sound is when all sing it correctly.

In the earlier exercises for warming up a choir, a variety of vowel sounds was used. This varied use will help singers learn to move to the correct formation with immediacy and to develop collective uniformity. During these exercises the conductor can relate the exercise to the texts of anthems that will be sung later in the rehearsal.

The syllables shown in Example 22 can be sung on the same pitch with emphasis on correct formation of the vowel, each group ending with the key words: *hut, her, hook,* and *hit, hut, heat.* The final syllable should be held to ascertain uniformity of vowel formations or to make whatever adjustments prove necessary. It is best to try for refinements on a group or section basis first. Only resort to individual refinements if necessary. Do not embarrass or alienate the individual singer.

Variations of these procedures should be improvised by the conductor.

When rehearsing an anthem, the conductor can also have the choir sing only on the vowel sounds without using any consonants. This will be difficult and amusing at first since singers are conditioned to articulate the consonants as they read the text for singing. However, stay with this procedure until the singers are able to sing only the vowel sounds. Concentration on the vowel sounds will help not only to improve the collective purity of vowel production, but also to enhance the blend of voices. In addition, it will enlarge the singers' sensitivity to uniform formation and assist them in maintaining good intonation.

Ex. 23: *Messiah* - "Since by Man Came Death"

The *Messiah* chorus, "Since by Man Came Death," is replete with the possibilities of pitch problems regardless of the size of the choir (see Ex. 23). Sometimes a quartet of soloists is used to forestall such problems, but poor intonation can often be heard even when just four voices sing. Intonation is always a special problem in slow-moving, unaccompanied, homophonic anthems. The following exercises will help to improve the tone quality and the blend of voices.

　　1. Have the choir sing the first three measures shown in Example 23 using only the vowel sounds. Employ a fermata on each chord. (Use a fermata on each of the following procedures.)

　　2. In measure 1, check the bass and tenor octave A.

　　3. In measure 2, check the tenor and soprano octave A and the bass and tenor octave D.

　　4. In measure 3, check the tenor and soprano octave C.

　　5. In measure 1, check the alto C and then the soprano E with the tenor and bass parts.

　　6. In measure 2, check the alto D with the tenor and soprano A and then with the bass F.

　　7. In measure 3, check the bass A with the soprano and tenor C and then add the alto E.

8. Sing measure 1 again and have two tenors sing the vowel *eh* instead of *ih*. Ask the choir to listen to the sound of the chord. Then repeat and ask the choir to listen for the change in intonation of the tenor section when the two tenors shift from *eh* to *ih*. This will make a choir very aware of the relationship of uniformly correct vowel formations to pitch accuracy and good intonation.

9. Sing each of the remaining chords with a fermata and check the pitches as in #8 above, but vary the parts in relation to any pitch problems that occur.

10. These exercises can be used in rehearsing any anthem, but some anthems may not require such careful attention. As pitch problems arise in rehearsals, the conductor may employ these exercises at some point during the preparation of the anthem.

In addition to helping intonation, these procedures can be used to enhance the tone quality and the blend of voices. As consonants are added, they can assist the singers in learning to arrive at the correct vowel sound with collective immediacy and unity.

When the setting of a text involves starting to sing with a vowel, as in Mozart's "Ave Verum Corpus," it is important that the breath be taken with the tongue, lips, and jaw in the correct vowel formation (see Ex. 24).

Ex. 24: Mozart - "Ave Verum Corpus"

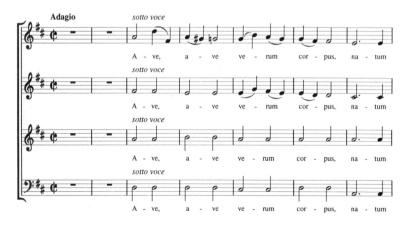

Singers should take the breath with the tongue, lips, and jaw in the *ah* position. Some may take the breath too late and never arrive at the *ah* position at the right time. Others may take it too early. All singers should take the breath rhythmically and at the right time with the help of the conductor's preparatory beat. Again, referring to the exercises on page 44 (*hip, hip, hoh, hah, haw, hee,* and so on), the unvoiced aspirated consonant *h* is used so that the mouth can form whatever vowel is to be sung. This disciplines the singers to be in the correct vowel formation before the vowel is sung on whatever pitch is assigned to it. The vocalises using *ee* and *ah,* and *ee, aye, ah, aye, ee* will also promote quick and precise movement to the correct vowel position. Thus, the vocalises help prepare the singers for whatever vowel formations are involved in anthems. (This will be discussed in more detail later.)

Ex. 25: *Messiah* - "And He Shall Purify"

The chorus in Example 25 demonstrates how singers must take a quick breath on the second beat of the first measure, with the lips, tongue, and jaw already in the formation of the vowel in the conjunction *and,* so that the vowel sound begins on the second half of the second beat. This chorus is replete with such entrances. It gives the singers ample discipline for rhythmic breathing coordinated with the proper vowel formation. It also gives conductors opportunity to practice providing correct preparatory beats or cues. Note the use of the word *practice,* for it should not be necessary to provide preparatory beats for every entrance in this chorus, but only as needed.

Consonants

Although most of the singing tone is produced by vowel sounds, consonants are necessary. Without consonants, the text of an anthem would not be intelligible. To prove this to the choir, the conductor should sing the words of a fairly familiar hymn using only the vowel sounds. Do not use the hymn tune, but sing the vowels on one pitch. A hymn like "A Mighty Fortress Is Our God" is a good choice. The conductor will have to practice this so that it can be done with ease. The tempo of the hymn must be used in the demonstration. Although choir members will find this amusing, only repeat it once if necessary. Most of the singers will not be able to detect what hymn you are singing, although there may be someone who hears the hymn.

Since the choir shares with the congregation the anthems it has prepared for worship, it is important that the congregation understand the texts. Whenever a choir sings, it represents the congregation. Thus, the choir not only sings *to* a congregation but also *for* the congregation, as choir and congregation worship God.

Since the singing tone is produced primarily by vowel sounds, many choir conductors spend most of the rehearsal time allotted to diction on vowel sounds. While work on vowels provides great assistance to the development of good vocal technique and the other benefits discussed above, to spend only token time on consonants overlooks and negates their significant contributions to refined singing. Consider the following contributions provided by consonants.

Consonants make possible graphic clarity of the text. Although vowels may be correctly and uniformly sung, if consonants are not carefully and correctly produced, the words will not be easily understood. Congregations should not have to guess what words are being sung.

Some consonants achieve pitch while others do not. The consonant chart shown in Figure 6 indicates those that can be voiced (achieve pitch) and those that are unvoiced (cannot achieve pitch). However, both groups can assist tone production.

The consonants that achieve pitch will receive longer duration in singing than in speech and the tempo will help determine the duration. Thus, the consonants underlined in Example 26 will receive longer duration because of the tempo.

Fig. 6: Consonant Chart

CLASSIFICATIONS	Voiced	Unvoiced		Manner of formation	Place(s) of formation
I. LABIALS	B	P		IP	L
	W	WH		FO	L
	M		NC	IP	L
II. LABIODENTALS	V	F	OC	F	LL/UT
III. DENTALS	D	T	OC	IP	T/UG
	TH	TH	OC	F	T/UT
	N		NC	IP	T/UG
	Z	S	OC	F	T/LG/MT
	ZH	SH	OC	F	T/MT/UG
	L		OC	F	T/UG
	J	CH	OC	IP	T/UG/MT
IV. PALATALS	R		OC	F	T/HP/MT
	NG		NC	IP	T/HP/MT
	Y		OC	F	T/HP/MT/LG
V. GUTTURALS	G	K(C)		IP	T/SP
	(kw) Q	Q (kw)		IP/F	T/SP/L
	(GZ) X	X(KS)	OC	IP/F	T/SP/LG/MT
VI. SIBILANTS	Z	S	OC	F	T/LG/MT
	ZH	SH	OC	F	T/MT/UG
	J	CH	OC	IP	T/UG/MT
VII. ASPIRATES		H		O	O
		WH		O	L
VIII. NASALS	M		NC	IP	L
	N		NC	IP	T/UG
	NG		NC	IP	T/HP/MT

O – oral: mouth in vowel position with little or nothing to impede the outward flow of air

F – fricative; the outward flow of air or sound is partially blocked by the position of the lips or the tongue

IP – both plosion and implosion involved in formation

L – lips
LL – lower lip
T – tongue

UG – upper gum line and ridge (alveolar) immediately above
LG – lower gum line
UT – upper teeth
MT – middle (upper) teeth
HP – hard palate
SP – soft palate, to the rear of the mouth behind the hard palate; velum

OC – oral continuant
NC – nasal continuant

Reprinted from *English Diction for the Singer* by Lloyd Pfautsch, Lawson-Gould Music Publishers, Inc. with permission.

Ex. 26: *Messiah* - "Since by Man Came Death"

In singing, the duration of most unvoiced consonants will approximate normal speech. However, there are exceptions related to tempo and these usually involve the dental sibilants *s* as in *cease*, *sh* as in *shush*, and *th* as in *think*. Completion of the word *since* involves the unvoiced dental *t* combined with the unvoiced *s*. The unvoiced consonants underlined in the same chorus in Example 27 will receive longer duration than in speech because of the tempo.

Ex. 27: *Messiah* - "Since by Man Came Death"

   Like those in Example 27, the consonants underlined in Example 28 are longer because of the tempo. The unvoiced *sh* in *surely*, the unvoiced *fs* in *griefs*, and the *s* in *sorrows* will receive longer duration when articulated in singing than in speech because of the tempo. Likewise, the voiced consonant *z* will receive longer duration as it completes the word *sorrows*.

   Ex. 28: *Messiah* - "Surely He Hath Borne Our Griefs"

The length of the duration will vary. To sing an *m, v,* or *z* requires longer duration than in speaking and is always related to tempo. By contrast, *b, d,* and *g* will have shorter duration of pitch, but will still have pitch. To articulate these consonants, pitch is involved, but will be of short duration.

It has already been pointed out that consonants will help singers use their breath to vitalize and sustain tone production. Example 29 shows how consonants can help provide support and vitality to a rising vocal line and also an increase in volume. The sopranos should flip the consonant *r* (giving it short pitch duration), add pitch to the voiced consonant *z* in the word *riseth* on D, and then sing the voiced consonant *l* in the word *light* (also on D) before moving to the vowel *ah* (the first half of the *ah-ih* diphthong in *light*) on the third beat. This will provide the support and vitality for the tone and also for the *crescendo*. The other sections should join with the sopranos in doing the same each time this ascending phrase is repeated.

Ex. 29: *Elijah* - "Blessed Are the Men Who Fear Him"

Sometimes, the conductor could ask that the consonant *l* be added on the F♯ since the sopranos might scoop or slide when moving from the D to the F♯. However, delaying the consonant *l* until the F♯ may cause excessive tongue tension, resulting in a tight or restricted vowel in the word *light*. The age, experience, and capabilities of the singers will help determine the ultimate decision after careful trial and testing of the possibilities.

There are initial, medial, and final consonants. Initial consonants begin a syllable or word, as in "O thou that tellest good tidings to Zion." Medial consonants come in the middle of syllables or words, as in "He watching over Israel, slumbers not nor sleeps." Final consonants complete a word, as in "O thou that tellest good tidings to Zion." In speaking and singing "that tellest," one articulation of the consonant *t* will both complete *that* and begin *tellest*. It would be incorrect to sing the consonant *t* twice. However, when the consonant *t* ends a word and begins the next word in a very slow tempo, then the *t* might be articulated twice.

Since singing involves producing vowel and consonant sounds of much more varied duration and greater range of pitches, care must be taken so that the vowel sounds begin on the note value assigned to a syllable or word. When a voiced consonant is sung, final consonants must be added at the end of the note value assigned to the syllable or word on whatever pitch is involved.

Ex. 30: *Messiah* - "For unto Us a Child Is Born"

In Example 30, the word *Wonderful* begins with the vowel sound *oo* (**u** as in *hoot*). The movement of the lips, tongue, and jaw to the vowel sound *uh* (ʌ as in *hut*) produces the consonant *w* sound. Do not move to the consonant *n* too soon! Be sure to give the vowel the duration of two sixteenth notes. It is helpful to repeat the *uh* (ʌ) vowel on the second sixteenth note ("Wuh-uhnderful") to help the singers achieve the proper duration. Then have them merely think about repeating the vowel while actually singing it for the duration of two eighth notes. The tongue moves to the upper teeth gum line to articulate both the *n* and the *d* just before the vowel in the second syllable, which will be very short. The consonant *f* will also be sounded just before the vowel in the final syllable. The consonant *l* will be added after the quarter note duration or on the third beat of the measure.

Failure to articulate final consonants correctly can be dangerous and even confusing as should be obvious in Example 31.

Ex. 31: *Elijah* - "Help, Lord!"

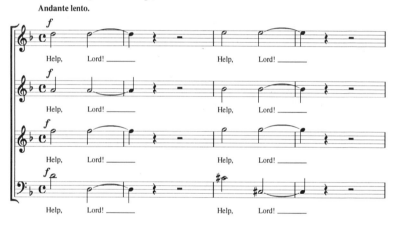

There should be a slight separation between the words *Help* and *Lord* so that the consonant *p* can be added and heard, and also that there will be time to sing the voiced consonant *l* before the third beat. Another comparable problem exists in Example 32.

Ex. 32: *Elijah* - "He Watching Over Israel"

The sopranos (and the rest of the choir) must be certain to use the voiced consonant *z* and *not* the unvoiced consonant *s* to complete the word *slumbers*. They should then add the consonant *n* on the same pitch before opening up on the vowel in the word *not*. It will be more difficult for the altos and basses since they must accomplish this within the duration of an eighth note. However, they are helped by moving on the same pitch.

The examples shown lead to one of the most important benefits of correctly articulating consonants: rhythmic accuracy and precision. Although many rhythmic problems are the result of failure to recognize and respect note values, most are related to inaccurate articulation of consonants—especially medial and final consonants. Starting an initial consonant too early or too late will obviously affect the rhythmic accuracy. Delaying medial and final consonants will cause sluggish rhythm flow. Adding medial and final consonants too quickly will push tempo and suggest an *accelerando*.

Ex. 33: *Elijah* - "And a Mighty Wind"

In Example 33, since Mendelssohn indicated *allegro con fuoco* for this chorus, the voiced consonants must be sung quickly so that

the fast tempo is maintained. Thus, the duration of the voiced consonants should not be stressed.

Handel indicated *allegro e staccato* in the chorus shown in Example 34. He wanted the words to be sung very quickly. In the first
measure, if the singers add the *t, s,* and *k* too quickly, the singers can
be "off to the races," leaving the conductor struggling to hold them
at a steady pace. In this instance, the duration of the vowels must be
stressed!

Ex. 34: *Messiah* - "Let Us Break Their Bonds Asunder"

Consonants contribute greatly to good vocal technique and healthy voices. When correctly articulated, they use only the amount of tension necessary for their production. When incorrectly articulated, they add unnecessary tenseness to the vocal production, whether it be in speaking or in singing, and this tenseness carries over into the vowel production and sound.

Conductors should work on correct consonant articulation constantly. It is hoped that, as with vowel formations, correct articulation of consonants will become habitual. Unfortunately, as with other vocal disciplines such as proper use of breath and resonance, singers in choirs will need reminders from their conductors who, in turn, must never "give up" or become easily satisfied with what they hear from their singers.

Some Results of Good Diction

- **Correct vowel formations will help the singers use their singing voice with greater ease and efficiency.**
- **Correct vowel formations will help the singers use their resonance potential to greater advantage.**
- **Correct vowel formation and articulation of consonants will help eliminate unnecessary and excessive tension.**
- **Correct vowel formation and the correct singing of voiced consonants will help intonation.**
- **Correct articulation of consonants will vitalize and help the breath to support tone production.**
- **Correct articulation of consonants can assist rhythmic accuracy and precision.**
- **Correct articulation of consonants can assist the control of dynamic gradations.**
- **Correct formation of vowels and articulation of consonants will provide clarity in singing the texts of anthems.**

CONCLUSION: GOOD DICTION IS THE KEYSTONE TO ALL GOOD SINGING AND EXEMPLARY CHORAL PERFORMANCES.

Chapter Four:
Achieving a Vital Choral Sound

Blend

Choir conductors talk about blend, they work on blend, and they tell their singers to work on blend, but they have different concepts of blend and how to achieve it.

In many college and university choirs, the members are selected according to the conductor's preconceived ideas about which voices will complement one another or blend easily without much effort being expended by the singers and conductor. In other choirs at this level, individual voices are selected as the "core" for the blend and all singers are arranged around that core to achieve the blend of voices desired. In many choirs, a homogeneous sound or blend will be developed under the guidance of the conductor, and the choir members will be selected on the basis of vocal quality, vocal production, vocal potential, and musicianship.

Church choir conductors work in different circumstances, since they must serve all members of a congregation who wish to sing in the choir. While there are obvious limitations, there is always a potential for which the conductor must constantly strive. Is the prospect for success impossible? Of course not! But achieving blend will take longer, and will be more difficult to achieve and sustain as a constant attribute of the choir's sound.

Put simply and succinctly, good blend is the result of vowel uniformity. By working on correct vowel formations, the conductor is not only helping the development of each voice in the choir, but the singers are also retaining their individuality or vocal identity. They do not have to sound like other singers. However, they must be encouraged (or commanded) to participate fully in the work on blend by using their lips, tongues, and jaws to form the vowels correctly, and by using their ears to hear their voice interacting with other voices in the choir.

As they join with the other singers in forming the vowel sounds correctly, their voices join to produce a combination of tone qualities that results in a blend that is unique to their choir. This blend will not necessarily be achieved in one rehearsal, one month, or even one season of the church year. But conductors may be surprised by how quickly this blend of voices can be achieved through patient, persistent work on correct and uniform vowel production. It will also be gratifying to the conductor as the faces of the singers show that they are not only hearing the difference, but also feeling the difference as a result of correct and uniform vowel sounds.

With good blend, no individual voices will dominate a section's sound or "stick out" as the choir sings. There will be four clearly defined sectional sounds and not a conglomerate of whatever number of voices make up the choir. The resonance potential of each singer will contribute to the resonance potential of the whole choir as a result of blend. It will be easier to work on other concerns such as intonation, consonant articulation, rhythmic accuracy, dynamics, balance of parts, melodic and verbal nuances, and anthem style or performance practice.

Intonation

One of the most persistent and difficult problems every choir conductor has to confront is poor intonation on the part of individual singers, which also affects the intonation of the choir. Keyboard performers do not have this problem because organs and pianos are tuned for them. If the organ and piano are not in tune, the performer is not at fault unless the performer forgot to have the instruments tuned. Instrumentalists have problems with intonation, but not as acutely as singers due to one basic difference: they do not have to form vowels and articulate consonants when producing the tones and pitches of their instruments.

Singers do not have valves or keys that can be pushed and they cannot place their fingers on the vocal folds to assist them in achieving the right pitches. Of course, the wind players have to push the right valves and keys for the pitches, and the shape and tension of their lips makes a difference. The string players have to develop fingering techniques so that they will place their fingers at the correct location on the strings for the required pitches. But they do not have to form vowels and articulate consonants!

There are many causes for poor intonation when singing. Here are some possible causes that choir conductors may encounter.

1. The ears of some singers are not sensitive to correct pitches and they do not hear their own faulty intonation.

Response: The choir conductor can help singers who have difficulty "hearing" pitches by placing them between two singers or in front of singers who do have good intonation. In warming up the choir, have the singers match pitches played on the piano using varied sequences like C-D-F-G-C, C-G-F-E-G-C, E-G-F-D-C, C-D-F-E-G, C-G-A-F-E-C-D, and so on. Conductors should improvise these sequences and make them increasingly more difficult.

Another possibility is playing an E and asking the singers to think a G before being directed to sing a G. This can be repeated on various pitches. Never move diatonically. It is important that different intervals be used and not repeated. If the problem continues, the conductor can ask the singer (or singers) to meet with her or him privately to develop ear sensitivity to pitch.

2. Singers use their breath improperly and fail to support pitch in their tone production.

Response: Use the z exercise referred to on pages 26-27 to make singers aware of the relationship of breath support to pitch.

3. Singers fail to relate individual pitch to that of the section.

Response: To help individual members of a section "join" the section pitch, have the whole section sustain the problem pitch and, after analysis of what the individual is doing incorrectly, suggest to the whole section what change or changes should be made. If this does not help, repeat what was said to the section but do so while looking directly at the individual singer with the problem. It may be necessary to do this several times. Have the rest of the choir listen and join with the conductor in rejoicing when the pitch becomes secure. The other sections can also learn from this vicarious involvement (and it also inhibits conversation!).

4. Sections fail to relate their intonation to that of the other sections.

Response: To help sections understand their responsibilities to one another for maintaining good intonation, utilize the suggestions on vowel sounds presented on pages 45-46.

5. There is general laxity in singing the third, fifth, and leading tone in a scale and also when singing whole and half steps.

Response: Have the choir sing in unison all of the intervals that are problems in the anthems being prepared. Although only one section may be having the problem, it is helpful to involve all of the singers for four reasons: (1) the section with the problem can be assisted and/or fortified by the other sections; (2) the section with the problem does not feel singled out or "on the spot"; (3) the interval involved will have to be sung at some time by every section; and (4) all sections are kept busy and involved.

6. Singers have too much tension in medial and final consonant articulation and they can continue this tension into the vowel sound, which may be either flat or sharp as a result.

Response: To relieve excessive tension in the tongue, jaw, and lips when articulating medial and final consonants, especially voiced consonants, isolate the consonant involved in the problem pitch or chord. Ask the choir to articulate correctly the consonant in speech. Then add the consonant to the rest of the word. If necessary, provide a model for the singers by demonstrating how the consonant should be articulated and ask the singers to emulate the model. When the singers have achieved correct articulation, add the pitch or pitches, but not without reminding them that the tempo and dynamics affect the length and intensity of the consonant articulation.

7. Singers are forming the vowels incorrectly and have too much tension in the tongue, jaw, and lips.

Response: The conductor should be sensitive to variations in the sounding of vowels. The ear should provide the first awareness. However, if the conductor looks at the singers it will also be possible to tell which singers are forming the vowels incorrectly. Frequently, the conductor, in an honest attempt to help the singers form the correct vowel, demonstrates with his or her mouth a formation that is wrong and the singers employ the same formation. Many teachers correctly advise conducting students not to "mouth the words for or with the singers." This is good advice for those conductors who tend to mouth the words throughout the whole anthem. However, an occasional reminder can be very effective in assisting the unity of vowel formation. Always provide this assistance just before a problem vowel would be formed by the singers. This is especially true when the choir has been consistently faulty in forming a specific vowel. (See the treatment of the word *amen* on pages 79-80.)

8. Too many singers have vibrato problems and these affect pitch.

Response: This will be discussed under "wobble trouble" in chapter 5.

9. The singers are victims of a poor acoustical environment.

Response: Intonation problems can be caused by poor acoustics, which make it difficult for singers to hear the organ or one another. Other factors are acoustical tile on the ceiling, thick carpeting covering the chancel and sanctuary floors, and heavily padded cushions in every pew. Since the singers have trouble hearing, they will sing out of tune. Patience and perseverance will be required to effect changes. Alert the music committee to the problem and solicit their understanding and support. Enlist the assistance of the musically enlightened members of the congregation. Seek help from a good church architect and an experienced acoustician. Good singing and intonation will always be enhanced by a favorable acoustical environment.

10. Lack of concentration by some or all of the singers in the choir causes poor intonation.

Response: All of the preceding responses involving suggestions for correcting causes of poor intonation require constant concentration on the part of singers and conductor. A conductor should never forget that lack of concentration can be a cause of poor intonation! Good intonation is one of the important attributes of superb choral singing. Unfortunately, while a choir conductor can spend a lot of limited rehearsal time working on good intonation, there is no assurance that all of the time and effort expended will result in good intonation.

Choirs are not organs or pianos. They are not wind or string instruments, which provide the instrumentalists some control over pitch and interval accuracy. Choirs are made up of human instruments, and choir conductors have very little control of pitch and intonation during a performance. Of course, there are a few conducting techniques or gestures that can help intonation, but these techniques and gestures cannot make a choir sing with good intonation. Even prayers to St. Cecilia, the patron saint of music, have often been to no avail! The conductor must work carefully and diligently on intonation in rehearsal with the hope that the concentration of the singers will carry over from rehearsal to service. It is also hoped that such concentration will become habitual.

Chapter Five:
Specific Choral
Concerns

Connecting Words

The connecting of two words, one ending with a vowel and the other beginning with a vowel, is a frequent problem in singing.

Ex. 35: *Messiah* - "For unto Us a Child Is Born"

In the chorus shown in Example 35, the connection between the words *unto* and *us* often sounds like "untowus," as if the consonant *w* came between the two words. The singers must be taught to end the *oo* (**u**) vowel in *unto* on the G and then move to the *uh* (ʌ) vowel in *us* on C without adding the *w* sound. There must be a slight separation between the *oo* (**u**) and the *uh* (ʌ) and a minimal glottal beginning of the second vowel sound *uh*. This will eliminate the consonant *w* sound. The same principle is operational in the additional examples from *Messiah*.

Ex. 36: *Messiah* - "O Thou That Tellest Good Tidings to Zion"

In Example 36, the connection between the words *say* and *unto* will require the same slight separation to eliminate "sayunto," with the *y* sounding like a consonant. Instead it should complete the diphthong *ehih* (ɛɪ), then move on the *uh* (ʌ). Or the vowel sound in the word *say* can be treated as the *a* (**e** as in *hate*) before moving on to the second vowel, which will receive a minimal glottal attack.

Ex. 37: *Messiah* - "Let All the Angels of God Worship Him"

In Example 37, the connection between the words *the* and *angels* will also require the same separation.

Ex. 38: *Messiah* - "Lift Up Your Heads, O Ye Gates"

In Example 38, the connection between the words *who* and *is* often sounds like "whowiz" and will also need a slight separation between the two vowels.

The connection between two words can also be problematic when the first word ends with a consonant and the second begins with a vowel.

Ex. 39: *Messiah* - "Glory to God"

In Example 39, the connection between the words *peace* and *on* often sounds like one word or "peason." The sibilant *s* must be added rhythmically and the sound stopped momentarily before opening up the *aw* (ɔ) vowel in the word *on* with the correct pitch.

Ex. 40: *Messiah* - "Hallelujah!"

In Example 40, there must not be a connection between the words *God* and *omnipotent.* The consonant *d* must be added quickly and the vowel *ah* (α), the first vowel in the word *omnipotent,* should be added after a slight separation.

There are instances of connections that involve a word ending in a consonant and the following word beginning with a consonant. In the chorus shown in Example 41, singers frequently give very short duration to the vowel in the word *good* and move immediately to the consonant *d*. This is hazardous because it can push the tempo. Since *d* is a voiced consonant of very short pitch duration, the singers tend to rush to the next word too soon. Some conductors try to solve this problem by having the choir sing these words (notes) *staccato.* An alternative is to have the singers sing "goo-dwill." Instead of connecting the *d* with the first vowel, connect it with the *w* at the start of the second word. This works rhythmically and gives correct duration to the first syllable. There is a danger that the singers might stress "dwill" too much. The conductor can negate this tendency by asking the singers to stress the first syllable and pull back from the second, especially since the connection involves an ascending interval. Note the marks above the two words in the example. Choral and vocal music is replete with such connecting problems and the suggested solution can usually be applied in most instances.

Ex. 41: *Messiah* - "Glory to God"

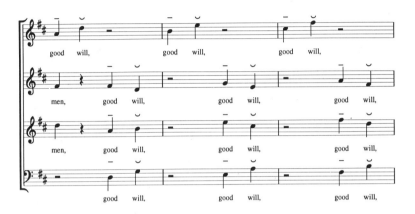

Ex. 42: *Messiah* - "And the Glory of the Lord"

In Example 42, it is only necessary to sing one *sh*, for it will complete the word *flesh* and also begin the word *shall.*

Ex. 43: *Messiah* - "And He Shall Purify"

In the chorus shown in Example 43, singers may have difficulty singing "that they." Tell the singers to move their tongues to the tip of the upper teeth as they did to sing the voiced consonant sound *th*, and then to articulate *th* in *they*. This one movement will complete the word *that* with the unvoiced consonant *t* and begin the word *they* with the voiced consonant *th* as in *this*.

The same movement of the tongue should be applied in connecting the words *behold* and *the* in Example 44. Since *d* is a voiced consonant, the pitch G must be given to the *d* and *th* in the word *the*. It helps to have the singers articulate the consonants *d* and *th* on the dot of the dotted eighth note. The vowel *uh* ($\land$) must begin on the sixteenth note.

Ex. 44: *Messiah* - "Behold the Lamb of God"

A very difficult connection occurs in Example 45 between the words *His* and *shoulder.*

Ex. 45: *Messiah* - "For unto Us a Child Is Born"

Here it is necessary to connect the voiced consonant *z* with the unvoiced consonant sound *sh.* This is difficult to do but the connection should not sound like "hisshoulder." There must be some *z* sound, which is a voiced consonant and achieves pitch, as well as the unvoiced consonant sound *sh,* and both are sounded during the duration of the sixteenth note.

Forming Vowels

The formation of some vowels differ in speech and in singing.

Ex. 46: *Messiah* - "And He Shall Purify"

In Example 46, many singers will sing the word *purify* to sound like "pureefy" although they would not use the *e* (i) vowel in speech, but rather the *uh* (ə) vowel. Indeed, the phonetic dictionary does give *uh* (ə)[1] for the second syllable, but if this were sung it

1. In speech, the (i) is for unaccented syllables of short duration and the (ə) is for accented syllables of long duration. Except in rare instances, singing requires longer duration of vowel sounds than in speech. Therefore, I have always preferred to use the (ə) in most instances, when this vowel sound is involved in a word or syllable.

would sound strange because singing elongates vowel duration and this is an unaccented syllable. Instead, ask the choir to sing the *ih* (I) vowel as in the word *hit.* This will eliminate the *e* (i) vowel and the result will be "purihfy," which is a much better sound than "pureefy" or "puruhfy."

Ex. 47: *Elijah* - "Cast Thy Burden upon the Lord"

In speech, most individuals would not put a vowel between the *d* and the *n* in the word *burden.* The phonetic dictionary gives "bɜdɛn" as the correct pronunciation. However, in Mendelssohn's setting (Ex. 47), the vowel is given pitch and duration of sound. As a result, at least three vowel sounds can often be heard when this chorale is sung. They are *ih* (I) as in *hit, eh* (ɛ) as in *head,* and *uh* (ʌ) as in *hut.* Conductors will have to decide which sound they desire. This writer has always preferred the use of *eh.*

Note Values

Singers frequently fail to sing words or syllables for the full note value, especially at the end of a phrase. This problem sometimes occurs in the "Hallelujah" chorus as shown in Example 48. The final syllable *jah* in the word *Hallelujah* usually receives a sixteenth note duration instead of an eighth note duration. As a result, singers often tend to rush or push the tempo. It also places too much syllabic stress on the final syllable, which is unaccented—or should be unaccented! A solution is to have the singers think two sixteenth notes (*yah-ah*) and hold the vowel for that duration. But they should not actually sing *yah-ah!* If absolutely necessary, the conductor can resort to having the choir sing *yah-ah,* which will help secure the proper duration of the vowel. But make it clear to the singers that they should not do this when actually singing the chorus.

Ex. 48: *Messiah* - "Hallelujah!"

Stressing the accented syllable *lu* (as Handel has done in this setting of the word) will also help negate this danger. Unfortunately, Handel may have predisposed singers to stress the first syllable throughout because during the first nine measures of this beloved chorus he put the first syllable *hal* on the first beat of the measure four times—but only four times. Yet most singers will continue to stress this first syllable throughout the chorus even though there is a preponderance of "hallelujah" settings with the accent on the third syllable. Conductors can train the singers to accent the third syllable as it should be, but not without a lot of work and determination. Most choirs have sung and will sing the word *hallelujah* with repeated accents on the first syllable. Tradition? Perhaps, but tradition can be broken and those who are not members of the choir probably will not notice the difference, especially if they are singing along, as they do in many churches. But it is possible to be faithful to Handel even in the four measures where the syllable *hal* begins on the first beat. Simply do not stress *hal,* but do stress *lu.*

Final consonant duration is often overlooked by many singers. The final note values are not observed.

Ex. 49: *Elijah* - "Behold God the Lord Passed By"

In Example 49, there must be a difference between the addition of the consonant *d* to the words *wind* and *Lord* and the consonants *ks* to the word *rocks.* Since this chorus is usually conducted in two, the *d* must be articulated on the second half of the first beat, whereas the *ks* consonants must be added on the second beat. But do not allow the singers to sing an eighth note for *wind* and *Lord.* Also, do not accept a quarter note duration for *rocks.*

Syllabic Nuance

Syllabic nuance is a common problem with singers and conductors. Stress is placed on unstressed syllables as the singers sing and as conductors conduct. Stress is also placed on unaccented syllables by composers.

Ex. 50: *Elijah* - "Cast Thy Burden upon the Lord"

In Example 50, the sopranos must be careful when they sing the second syllable in the word *burden.* The ascending interval can cause them to stress the second syllable. They must stress the first syllable and diminish the tone and stress slightly as they move from the G to the C.

Ex. 51: *Messiah* - "Hallelujah!"

The problem of syllabic nuance can be shown in the "Hallelujah" chorus in Example 51. Many choirs stress the first syllable when singing the word *hallelujah,* with *jah* receiving a secondary accent. This is not correct. The accent should be on the third syllable *lu,* just as Handel has set the word. While Handel was not as sensitive to syllabic accents in English as Purcell was, he was especially successful in *Messiah.* However, there is another example where conductors and singers have to make subtle adjustments in nuance to negate the tendency to stress an unaccented word and syllable.

In the chorus "He Trusted in God that He Would Deliver Him," singers must sing the words "He trusted in God" without equal stress on each syllable, as one often hears in *Messiah* performances. The words should be sung as indicated in Example 52.

Ex. 52: *Messiah* - "He Trusted in God that He Would Deliver Him"

Example 53 shows the need for nuance even when eight voices are singing and the dynamic level is *forte*. The first soprano must not stress the conjunction *and,* but lighten up as she moves from the E to the G before the climax of the phrase on the word *guide*. Likewise, the baritone must be very careful when he moves from the G on the word *hold* to the C for the conjunction *and*. He too must lighten up as he joins the second tenor in unison on the C and then moves through the B to the climax of the phrase with the rest of the singers on the word *guide*. This may seem like a minor consideration, but such careful attention to nuance and balance adds to performance standards.

All careful work on correct vowel formations and correct articulation of consonants should lead to sensitive and subtle verbal and melodic nuances. The choir conductor has to provide guidance for the singers by indicating which syllables or words should be stressed, by vocal demonstrations, and ultimately in the conducting gestures.

Ex. 53: *Elijah* - "He Will Give His Angels a Charge"

Problem Words

There are three words that all church choirs have to sing, and very few ever do so correctly. They are: *Lord, God,* and *Amen.* When singing the word *Lord,* some singers make it sound like "lard," while others end up with "lohrd." To help singers sing this word correctly, have them sing the vowel sound *aw* (ɔ) as in *awful.* Ask them to sing the vowel sound *uhr* (ɜ) as in *her.* Then put the two sounds together as in *awuhr,* but keep the tip of the tongue against the lower gum line and do not let it curve up to the roof of the mouth! The consonant *r* is not pronounced in this word, but merely contributes to the spelling and joins with the written *o* to form a syllable that contains the *awuhr* diphthong. The voiced consonant *d* completes the word. But if the tongue moves up too soon, the "Midwestern" or "American" *r* will be heard. It will take time to achieve collective agreement.

When singing the word *God,* some singers sound like they are singing "Gahd," and others, "Gawd." An easy way to correct this is to have all singers sing an *ah* (ɑ) vowel, as in *father,* correctly. Then ask them to sustain this sound while rounding the lips slightly without changing the tongue and jaw position. This will result in a uniform sound.

When singing the word *Amen,* some singers will sing an *uh* (ʌ) vowel for the first syllable and others will sing *aw* (ɔ). The first group of singers have not lowered their jaws far enough and the second group is rounding their lips. Have all singers yawn and stress that the jaw should be in this low position. Then it is necessary to point out that the lips must be relaxed since they do not contribute to the formation of this vowel and thus there should be no rounding of the lips.

Another problem that occurs when singing the word *Amen,* involves the consonants. The pitch duration of the voiced consonants *m* and *n* must be added to the vowel sounds in relation to the tempo. The consonant *m* should complete the *ah* vowel and also begin the *eh* vowel sound; for example, *ahm-mehn* and not *ah-men* or *ahm-en.* If the word *amen* is sung on the same pitch, it is as if the consonant was elongated (*ahmmmmen*). When two pitches are involved, the consonant *m* is added to the *ah* vowel and the *eh* vowel begins the next pitch.

Ex. 54: "Amen"

Since the *m* and *n* are voiced consonants (achieve pitch), the *m* continues the G chord in the first measure until the *eh* vowel begins the D chord, and the *n* completes the syllable on the D chord. The same is true in the next measure in the E and B chords. In the third measure, the *m* sounds on the D chord before moving to the final G chord, which begins with the *eh* vowel. The *n* finishes the G chord on the downbeat eighth note or it can be added on the fourth beat of the final measure. Be sure to give it enough duration of pitch (though not excessive).[2]

Wobble Trouble

Conductors of church choirs have to deal with "wobble trouble" or vibratos that widen as singers grow older. Another aspect of the

2. Some publishers are actually adding an eighth note tied across the bar line to a quarter, half, or whole note that ends a phrase. This is done to ensure that the singers and conductors will sustain the note to full value before adding the consonant on the eighth note. It may also be that they think conductors and singers are not intelligent enough to give proper duration to the note value.

aging process is inadequate use of the breath for support and stability in tone production. All of the muscles used and needed for singing gradually lose their vigor or tone (not pitch), and this results in changing vibrato characteristics. Most singers have a vibrato in their tone production and all vibratos have the following characteristics:

- There will be two pitches involved.
- There will be variance in the two pitches involved.
- There will be variance in the width between the two pitches involved.
- There will be differences in the speed at which these two pitches are sung.
- One of the two pitches will dominate either by volume, by duration, or by both volume and duration.

A good way to test the vibrato is to use a reel-to-reel tape recorder. Record the singer at the regular speed (7 1/2). The singer will hear his or her own voice. Then play the tape again at half speed (3 3/4). This will surprise the singer because the sound will be much lower. It will also clearly disclose that two pitches are involved, how fast (or slow) these two pitches are sounded, the width of the intervals between the pitches, the dominance of one pitch over the other (although this can change in the singing process), and whether the dominance is by volume or duration of pitch.

There are several ways to address the wobble problem. Persistent work on breathing exercises is an obvious first step. Then it is essential that the breath be connected with tone production in a vital way (refer back to exercises using the consonant *z* in chapter 2). The singers can be asked to sing a "straight tone." However, in trying to produce a "straight tone" their vibratos will become faster, the intervals will be smaller, and the two pitches will have more equal stress and duration. But do not expect this result on the first attempt, and when successful do not assume that it will be habitual. The conductor will have to repeat the process over and over until the problem is corrected.

Lack of controlled vibratos does affect pitch. While a lot depends on the factors just discussed, even well-trained voices can present problems with their vibrato characteristics. So much depends on which of the two pitches is dominant and which pitch is "true pitch." When checking vibratos, a conductor can often learn that the cause for flatting is related to the fact that the singers begin on "true pitch" but the next pitch in the vibrato is low. This would not be so problematic if the vibrato is fast and the interval tight. But if the lower pitch is also dominant both in volume and duration, the pitch will be flat.

By contrast, singing sharp occurs when the singers begin on "true pitch" but the next pitch in the vibrato is high. This is often the result of a fast vibrato and will show up when sopranos and tenors sing in their high range. The vibratos of famous singers will always show that they are not consistent in beginning on "true pitch" but will vary, especially in relation to range and tessitura. The testing with the reel-to-reel tape recorder will be helpful in making these differences obvious. Unfortunately, cassette tape recorders do not provide us with the ability to change speeds as suggested above.

Ultimately, it is helpful if conductors develop their aural sensitivity so that they can hear these differences as they listen to singers. Then they can arrive at the correct diagnosis of the vibrato problem and make appropriate suggestions to encourage the singers to correct the problem. A conductor cannot and should not just complain about intonation, ask the singers to "tune it," or call out "you're flat" or "you're sharp." The suggestions submitted under "intonation" on pages 61-63 may be of assistance, but do not overlook the role played by vibrato characteristics.

No Vibrato

In contrast to "wobble trouble," it is currently fashionable among many church choir conductors to insist that the singers use a "straight tone" production with no vibrato. This can result in better or more secure intonation. It would be stylistically correct for anthems of the English cathedral tradition, but it would not be correct for a motet by Brahms. In other words, judicious use of "straight tone" production is warranted, but not as a constant choral demand.

Use of this vocal technique at all times can be injurious to the vocal mechanism of mature female voices because of the abnormal tensions required to produce this atypical sound by mature singers. Repeated use of the "straight tone" can be as taxing as it is tiring on the human instrument. Singers who have had private lessons may rebel against this technical demand and the more gifted singers may quit singing in the choir. However, they will usually cooperate occasionally because of an anthem's style, but not if it is expected throughout every rehearsal. To employ a specific vocal technique for a particular style of anthem is as necessary as it is appropriate. But to apply a specific vocal technique to all anthems is antipathetic to varied styles.

Addenda

If a choir conductor has employed breathing exercises and stressed the use of resonance but is still not satisfied with the sound of the voices, try this quick "cure." Ask the singers to stand and then bend forward and let their arms hang freely. Then have them sing the vocal line that needs more support and more head resonance. The support and resonance will be there! Why? Because they are forced to use their breath correctly, supporting the tone from the lower rib cage. They will not only use more head resonance, they will also feel the resonance. And what is of ultimate importance, they will hear the difference as well as feel the difference. Often, it is best to do this by sections so that those who are not singing can hear the change objectively and applaud the accomplishments.

Every choir conductor must work with the singers in such a way that their voices are helped and not hindered. Vocal technique should be developed and not restricted. The singer's love of singing should be encouraged and not discouraged. Singing in a choir should be exhilarating, satisfying, and fulfilling—both vocally and musically.

Choral therapy is an endless process. But as a conductor helps the singers use their voices more correctly and efficiently, conductors and singers are enabled to share choral music at a higher level of artistry and beauty. And the singers will have healthier voices!

Glossary

Actuators—The diaphragm, lower ribs, lungs, intercostal muscles, and abdominal muscles that begin and control the movement of air from the thorax to the larynx.

Alveolar ridge—A portion of the roof of the mouth that is between the gum line of the upper teeth and the beginning of the hard palate.

Articulation—The action of the lips, lower jaw, and tongue in making possible the necessary vowel and consonant sounds needed to make words intelligible.

Articulators—The lips, lower jaw, and tongue that move to requisite positions for the formation of vowels and the production of consonants.

Aspirate—Unvoiced consonants produced by the outward flow of air as in "*he*" and "*wh*om."

Breath support—The use of the breath supply in the lungs after inhalation to effect the vibration of the vocal cords with sufficient stability and vitality to produce various pitches at different dynamic levels.

Consonants—Vocal sounds produced by the articulatory movements of the lips, lower jaw, and tongue, which interrupt and add to the flow of vowel sounds to make words intelligible.

Continuant—A consonant sound that has duration of clarity and quality, whether voiced or unvoiced.

Dentals—Consonants that are articulated by action of the tongue against the upper teeth, the upper gum line, or alveolar ridge.

Diaphragm—A partition of muscle and connective tissue separating the thorax from the abdomen. The diaphragm moves down and intercostal muscles move outward as the principal muscles of inhalation. This results in an expansion of the thoracic and abdominal cavities. Figure 1 on page 15 shows the diaphragm in its relaxed state. These muscles combine to provide breath support for speaking and singing.

Diphthong—A combination of two vowel sounds in one syllable. In singing, the first vowel is sung for most of the note value to which the syllable is assigned and the second vowel is added just prior to leaving that note value.

Enunciation—The production of vowels and consonants with emphasis on clarity and distinctness.

Epiglottis—An elastic cartilage behind the tongue and above the larynx that covers the glottis during swallowing.

Final consonant—A consonant that is articulated at the end of a word.

Glottal—Articulated or produced by the glottis.

Glottis—The opening between the vocal cords.

Gutturals—Consonants that are articulated by action of the back of the tongue against the soft palate where it connects with the hard palate.

Hard palate—That part of the roof of the mouth that comes between the alveolar ridge and the beginning of the soft palate.

Initial consonant—A consonant that begins a word.

Intercostal—The muscles between the lower ribs.

Labials—Consonants that are articulated by the use of the lips.

Labiodentals—Consonants that are articulated by the lips in contact with the upper teeth.

Laryngopharynx—A portion of the pharynx just above the larynx.

Larynx—A structure of muscles and cartilages in which the vocal cords are located at the top of the trachea.

Melodic nuance—The stress of words and syllables in relation to the contour of the melodic lines or intervals between pitches.

Nasals—Continuant consonants using head resonance.

Nasopharynx—The portion of the pharynx located above the oropharynx in the nasal passages.

Nuance—The stress of syllables and words to enhance the expression or meaning of words in a text.

Oropharynx—The portion of the pharynx that is between the soft palate and the epiglottis.

Palatals—Consonants that are articulated by action of the tongue moving to the roof of the mouth or hard palate.

Pharynx—A portion of the alimentary canal connecting the mouth and nasal passages to the larynx and esophagus.

Phonation—The production of vocal sounds in speech or in singing.

Phonetics—Symbols representing speech sounds and their production (or formation and articulation).

Posture—The bearing or carriage of the body related to the purpose of the position.

Pronunciation—The sound and accent of words as usually spoken by those who are qualified to serve as models.

Resonance—The quality imparted to vocal sounds by the resonating potential of the pharynx, oral cavity, and nasal cavities of each human being, and thus unique and distinctive.

Sibilants—Consonants that have a hissing or buzzing sound when articulated.

Soft palate (or velum)—A soft membrane connected to the hard palate toward the back of the mouth.

Speech intoned—A description of singing.

Strident—Tone production that has a harsh quality with too much hard palate resonance.

Syllabic nuance—The accentuation or stress of syllables within words in order to enhance the expression or meaning of the words in a text.

Tessitura—The average range of a melodic line or voice part.

Thoracic—Related to, located within, or involving the thorax.

GLOSSARY

Thorax—The upper part of the body, which is a cavity between the neck and the abdomen.

Trachea—That part of the respiratory tract through which air moves for inhalation and exhalation.

Tremolo—A vibrato that is excessively wide and slow.

Triphthong—A word or syllable requiring the combination of three vowel sounds with the first vowel receiving the longest duration in relation to the note value assigned to the syllable. The second and third vowels are added just before leaving that note.

Unvoiced consonant—A consonant that does not (and cannot) achieve pitch when the voice is singing.

Vibrato—A slight and rapid fluctuation between two pitches in producing the singing voice.

Voiced consonant—A consonant that achieves pitch when the voice is singing.

Vowels—A group of speech sounds that are the most prominent part of a syllable. In singing, they differ from speech in that they achieve more varied pitches, the range of the pitches is much broader, there is a greater variety in the duration of their sound, and the dynamic levels are much broader when vowels are sustained.